PARAS YADAV

Letter from an outcast

First edition

ISBN: 978-93-5525-713 0

This book was professionally typeset on Reedsy.
Find out more at reedsy.com

for the mirror:
it says nothing, and says everything.

a brain may die, yet ideas live on.
bury them if you must —
they refuse to decompose,
and someday they're found as trea-
sure.

PARAS

Contents

Trial

I have committed crimes —
who will punish me?
Confession lives in my chest,
my heart sits as jury.

Every night, when the moon keeps watch,
and sometimes by the noon sun,
they charge me —
one by one, loud in my skull.

No seat is offered — I stand in a bare circle.
My legs tremble; mercy has made no plans.

I'm hated as a victim;
I plead as defendant —
fighting on both sides,
while my lawyer stays absent.

The counting dulls;
  the gallery is thin and terrible.
  A few seats fill with visitors —
  they've come to cheer my death,
  or curse me if I walk free.

Silence makes the room cold;
  my blood tastes metallic.
  The courtroom settles inside my head —
  the visitors are my other names;
  many wear my face.

Sometimes I am the victim,
  sometimes the accused —
  responsible for my deeds.
  So who will punish me?

My peace shivered in warmth

Sometimes, on wild nights —
  cold, as if the night had died;
  no wind reaches my soul.
  They stay out, blocked by a few high walls;
  they couldn't climb them — they stalled.

I stay inside, sitting at the table.
  The clock keeps hush, then bangs;
  I notice nothing — not even the moon.
  Except for my diary; it stays in my hand —
  its spine cracked, smelling of ink.
  I clutch it and pray it never ends.
  She stays with me in every word,
  in every crooked letter I write;
  even my faulty lines — she keeps them all.

But today — everything just feels so wrong.
  I carry my jacket as usual,

but the night is warm — I won't put it on.
Maybe the weight I carry in my thoughts
weighs me down.

I want to say it all to my darling,
yet my fears hold me back —
afraid of being judged, afraid of being misunderstood.
I don't know why today — I have it all.
I close them and all the ink dries away.

When the music ends

I want to dance
  Will you lead me onto the stage?
  Hold my hand with a tight grip —
  don't let me fall,
  don't let me fade.
  I promise I won't miss a step,
  even if my legs grow old
  or falter for reason unknown.

Darling, hold me close,
  your arm at the nape of my neck.
  Look into my eyes —
  then into the mirror
  that always craves your smile.

Trust me with this night;
  leave the world behind.
  I won't make it long,

nor make it brief —
just enough for both of us
to carry grief when all ends.

I want to dance with you,
and later, with the memories,
until my deathbed.

To look inside

Today, I lost this war —
  one I practiced for,
  but never fought.
  A letter waited
  in my mailbox.

"It said, 'It's over.
  Why weren't you home?
  They called your name,
  begged for your hand,
  but you were gone —
  lost in the cruelty outside,
  forgetting the one
  who waited within four walls.'"

I put the letter down,
  looked at the floor.
  Blood pooled at my feet —

the floor a red map of what I'd missed;
my eyes alone stayed black,
to witness the darkness grow.

I turned to the glass and looked within –
the rooms of me were a mess.
A cloud ran wild, turning black –
it left no trace of white.
Old thunder, my inheritance,
rolled through the room,
and I felt it crawl out of me.

The good in me,
once complaining out,
now choked on silence –
i was a saint gone blind
inside his own house.

The Storm came back

Today the storm came back.
Winds sang their old, thin melodies,
dancing across my roof.
They seemed to love the rain.
I stayed afraid.
The night turned cold —
as if I'd woken at the North Pole
with no soft snow to soften the world.
The wind shouted, screaming all around.

I zipped my jacket up to my chin —
all warm, and yet I'd forgotten my socks.
I climbed to the rooftop.
Your house was the first my eyes sought.
They searched for you. You weren't there.
Why did you have to leave?

A minute — or a decade — passed.

The wind changed; its voice broke.
Tears fell — maybe from the sky,
maybe from something that lost its way
They missed someone, the way I miss you.
People call it rain; some danced, some forgot.
Was that the same path I walked?

Then my legs went numb, pure white — no red,
the cold a slow, bright forgetting.
I had left my socks behind; I had kept your scent.
I was so lost in you, I forgot what warmth meant.

The Potter

Picking up his sword,
  the soldier looked to the sky —
  pictured his mother, his wife,
  then met the eyes
  of the potter of his life.

That brave, ruined soldier wore scars
  on his soul, and the pot the potter had made
  bore the same marks.
  They seemed to bleed; yet no blood fell.
  Something other — a strange, holy flow — moved there:
  tears of heaven, bright as the sun,
  fell and never quite reached the earth.

The connection came: the potter saw him.
  He joined his hands and dropped to his knees,
  though the knees themselves were where it hurt.
  Before he could open his mouth or let a word slip,

he blinked once — then, without another sound, asked,
"Meaning?"

The potter felt it all.
He understood the whole small novel,
framed in one word.
He looked at his hands, then at the clay turned red.
His tears were the last to fall —
and so it ends.

Terrible painter

He who painted us
botched the work.
Lines bent where they should have been straight,
borders melting into maps of ruin.
Greed moved first; kindness bled last.
Dear Painter — you did the colours wrong,
Painted blood red where life needed green.
Behead the green, and the air grows thin;
and we choke on what the world has lost.

Me and the Watcher

Looking up at the night sky,
I see the moon — bright,
lying in a field of dark.
Around you, scattered companions — the stars.
I wonder who else is gazing at you,
and what you cast upon their pages.
In their eyes, what do you look like —
a mess, or something that matters?
Maybe a friend — or just another cold rock.

Oh Moon —
you've watched enough of what happens down here.
You've heard their stories. How did they treat you then?
Were they kinder once, or is the present the same?
Tell me what the king said when he was made to beg.
What became of the dwarf when he rose like a mountain?
But most of all — do you miss any of them?

Ugly in eyes

It was beautiful,
Until it became ugly.
It was good,
Until it turned bad.
It was love,
Until it made us strangers.

It changed so quickly,
I didn't even get to question
The intentions it had hidden.

The beauty turned ugly—
Or maybe the lens shifted,
Because the person never did.

The good became bad—
Was it ever understood?
Or are the mistakes happening now,

Quietly, without witness?

And the love—
Ah, the love…
The poet watched,
Silent,
As it slipped away.

A madman

Sometimes... every day
  when I think of you
  in the deepest hour of night
  or under soft, early sunlight—

your lovely smile bends the morning sun,
  your ocean-deep, black eyes
  pull me in,
  until I shrink—
  a madman,
  drowning in devotion.

I know how to swim,
  yet still,
  I never dare.

YOU

If I ever again get to smile
truly, with no ache behind my lips.
If I ever get to breathe
and feel it fill me with life again.
If I ever get to see
And believe in what I see.
If I ever get to dream again
I'll, want it to be you,
Wrapped in the sheets, of bloom
Addressed under forever
Where goodbyes will mean nothing
And we remain
Like the moon and the earth
Held in orbit by sun.
Far, but never truly apart
Always circling.
Always home.

Goodbye

Are you happy? Finally,
Somewhere where no voices ache,
Where everything glows
And light stays.
Please be as you are,
Smiling through all the bright days.
When night arrives on clouds,
Close as the rabbit in your arms—
Let the mist rain, heavy and loud,
Reflecting the joy in those two eyes.

They were cute when I looked in them;
They felt like shelter for my storms,
A home for my torn pockets
And my perished fate—
Where rent didn't matter.
I had found a sun
Who would keep me warm

Through all the chilling summers.

I…
it's good here.
I'm learning to be.
Please be happy where you are.
Goodbye.

I am in peace

I am in peace—
At least, that's what I see.
All around me: tall trees,
Beautiful grass, the moon, the stars,
And the sun—God, I don't want to miss it.

But it was never really here.
The bulb glows each night,
Flickering through every shadow.
But light?
It never came—
Maybe it just bounced
Off the walls of space.

Was it my curse?
Or am I the demon of pain—
Always wrong,
Always in the wrong faith?

But rest assured,
  I won't say it again.

I'm in peace.
  I'm in peace.

Yet still—
  The wildfires rage around me.
  That's all I see.

Forgive me, but i breathe

One day, I'll smile.
One day, these stars will rise—
They'll stop twinkling
and roar like lions,
like a never-ending fire.
A volcano, a meteor,
melting frozen time.

They'll burn off all my scars—
deep,
but not wide.

Maybe I carry hope
somewhere
that never existed,
not in this crowd of cowards.

Maybe they rage at me

for my crime of stealing
a few breaths—
just one or two, I guess.

If it hurts you all—
if it chokes your lungs
and aches your heart,
then I'll take a bus.
If not,
I'll Walk.
Far from your zones—
your tables,
your beds,
your huts where you sleep.

But forgive me—
I'll never stop.
I can't.

The chariot's call

The bell rings
When the chariot arrives.
Pain, sorrow—everything hides,
And a dull smile drift
To every corner of this circle,
Dead-alive, like a blind man.

I was there when they last arrived.
It was my home—
At least, I called it mine.
I remember it as *the place*—
Where I first learned to speak,
The only place where words brought claps.

A zone of pure—
A circle, small yet wide.
And the smile was all I saw,
Until one day I reached my height

And realized—
It was all a painted lie.

But it doesn't matter now.
I'm a tall boy.
This was the conversation
I had with myself
In the circle's corner
When the chariot arrived.

The bells were ringing.
And there, I said
To this place I once called home—
Goodbye.

RED HUT

Somewhere, deep in distant lands,
blue water folds itself around them.
Roses swim there—
struggling to survive,
pleading to remain alive,
though fate has already marked them for death.

I own a hut in that place.
Small. Red.
Built from bush and white flames,
its edges forever caught in fire.
I live there,
and call it home.

No one comes.
No one ever has.
I breathe only dust—
ash woven into every inhale.

I drink poison
until it settles in my blood,
dragging me into a haze.

It drives me to run,
to dream of flight,
to reach above and beyond.

But when I fall,
plunging into that ocean,
the roses are there—
all dead,
whispering their goodbyes
for another life.

Only a Sweat, please—Goodbye

The story is real—
One I've longed to narrate.
Only the character? That, I fake.
What I say
Is always the poison I take,
The drink I choose.

In the air,
Even the ocean floats—shrinking deep,
Holding false hopes,
Yet somehow it breathes.
Masks on, sweating heavy—
That's what I see.
That's what eats me.

In my dream,
Too big, yet far too small.
Wide—yet narrow.

A tree, but no taller than a shrub.

Hey, hey, hey—
I know,
It's hard.
But I wrote what I held.
No more texts.
No more lines.

Only a sweat,
Please—
Goodbye.

Sun waits for the night lady

The sun waits for the night lady—
  a paradox in motion,
  a rusty chain turning the hours,
  rude and polite all at once.

I lived in that same cycle,
  spinning through its turns,
  until, one day, it stopped—
  or perhaps I stopped caring.

In the tales of earth and moon,
  I found my star upon a shore.
  She wore a crown,
  a flower tucked in her hair,
  her hands scattering glitter in the air.
  Her eyes—vast, unblinking—
  met my small world.

The sun abandoned me,
  and the sky dimmed with timid stars,
  but she stood,
  the steady pole of my heavens.

I walked toward her,
  love beating red through my veins,
  her scent pulling the breath from me—
  I was walking on air.

Soon, I was near enough
  to feel the warmth of her skin.
  She took my hand,
  and I was hers entirely.

Then, the sun that once left me
  returned for us both.

Still Inhaling Your Dust

Even after all these years,
  Of trembling fears
  And too many tears—
  You still visit me.

Sometimes in our room,
  The one we made,
  In that house we called ours.
  Sometimes,
  You come as a tree—
  Alone, bare, and leafless.

That tree is me.
  Alive, but hollow.
  Trying to breathe,
  But there's no air left.
  Hungry,
  But every meal slips off the table.

Everything I say feels unfinished,
Like something buried too deep to reach.
It's all new to me,
Just like our love once was.

But this time,
I bear it alone.
Your goodbye—
A farewell I never accepted.

I only want to know,
So tell me—
How did you forget it all,
When I'm still here,
Inhaling your rusty dust?

I have a name

I have a name—
Call me with that.
It sounds heavy,
Though it's barely wide.

I live in the rain, beneath the sun,
Cotton shields drape me from a world gone numb.
I drink this air—
It swims up and around,
Sometimes down,
Sometimes kissing the ground.

It fuels me,
For the name I wish
Would echo—loud and wide.

There is water too.
Sometimes.

Rarely.
Only when the drought of blue
Waves a fading goodbye.

In that moment, I inhale pure AQI,
And find no humans—
They've long died.
Too naive to even witness life.

Wonders still amaze us,
This circus we made for us—
A show where animals walk free,
Though they no longer have feet.

I have a name—
Heavy, not wide.
Call me with that.
Because I refuse to carry
The lies of your borrowed identity.

Evening Eyes

Evening eyes
  Gazing at the sky,
  Realizing this world is a lie—
  Painted blue, then white,
  Sometimes red,
  But mostly, it hides in black

Evening eyes of mine,
  Shrinking in tears,
  Floating, barely swimming.
  They cried out loud—
  Screaming high above the ground.
  But no hands reached down.
  Maybe they feared the dirt.
  Or maybe,
  They just liked to watch me drown.

Whatever is the cause

I simply don.t wanna pause

Evening eyes—
Drowning in hope
That a savior might arrive,
A faceless hero, cloaked in light…
But no one ever came.

And years later,
The tears dried on their own,
Burned away by the sun—
A cruel kindness of time.
And those same eyes,
Once sunk and soaked,
Grew hands of their own—
To wipe the flood away.
Themselves.

Tight black hug

There's a magic in my blood—
some call it curse; it stains me black,
folds me into shadow, steals my shape
when night takes its slow parade.

They call me son of darkness—
maybe that's what the sun believes.
I asked him once, "Mr. Sun, point me somewhere
where no one can find me."
He scolded me for cowardice,
said I should stand in his light.

He never saw what I carry under skin—
dullness, lines, a quiet ruin that refuses to burn.
His light runs off my bones like water;
it never learns the hollows I keep.

Then one pale day I met him—

a shadow smiling with white teeth.
He touched my face; a single tear
fell, impossible, and bright.
I let it be the only truth I kept.

NORTHERN GATES

As the clock on my wall
Strikes its final note,
And that dissonant melody
Beats against my chest—
I will vanish from this world.
No crime stained my hands,
No blood marked my soul,
Yet I will disappear
Like a ghost in plain sight.

Why? Am I weak? Am I small?
No—I feel strength within.
So why this urge to flee?
Because I despise this dust:
The hollow voices,
The hollow hearts,
Men who worship echoes of themselves,
Playing victims in empty rooms.

Some brandish swords in God's name—
Tell me, does heaven need their war?
Some chase hollow fame—
Born to nothing, proud of less.

I will not write their novel.
Just these few lines:
I long to slip away
To the plains beyond the gates—
Where men are human, not beasts,
Where life is real, not a lie.

There, my restless heart will rest,
My endless shuffle stilled—
In a world of truth, not false dreams,
At the northern gates, I'll live—and breathe.

Also by Paras Yadav

Not a Fairytale